KNOWING

HEARING

&

OBEYING

GOD'S VOICE

DR. STACIE BRYANT

To my dearest friend Sharon, from Linda

CONTENTS

Chapter One

Chapter Two

Chapter Three

Chapter 1

Knowing God's Voice

As a mother of six children I have heard them often tell me that they know something before it is fully explained to them. I would become furious with them when they would say they know something that they really didn't because I wasn't allowed to finish my sentence. My kids know when I am angry with them by the tone of my voice. They know my voice when I call them by phone or when I would call them through our home intercoms. The idea is that my kids are familiar with my voice and according to my voice they know which way to respond to me. However, if they prevent me from speaking they won't know my voice. My infant daughter knows my voice and looks around to find me if I am speaking in the same room. The point is my children know my voice and if we are all God's children we should know His voice. John 10: 4-5(paraphrased) states that as God's sheep He goes before us and we follow Him because we know His voice. It further states that because we know the voice of the father we won't follow after a stranger's voice, but we will flee because we don't know the voice of a stranger. The word "know" is defined as to be acquainted with, to be able to distinguish; recognize as distinct, and to discern the character or nature of. I take these definitions literal in my relationship with God and knowing His voice.

To be Acquainted with God is to *Know* Him

You can't expect to know God if you are not acquainted with Him. In order to become acquainted with Him you must be willing to spend time with Him. It is not always easy to find the right place and time to spend quality time with God to get to know Him. As a mom and wife I often feel pulled in a million directions. My children are India (23), Marquise (21), Diamante (18), Asia (16), Blake (3), and Tamar (3months). I am also married to an active duty Air Force Officer. I am a Marriage Family Therapist with a PhD in Psychology who often gets called on for emergencies. As a therapist, in private practice, I live by the constraints of time. Essentially, I live by schedules and the time allowed between work, kids, and wife duties. In my spiritual life there is not a scheduled set time for me to spend with God to keep my acquaintance with Him. I think that God has a sense of humor because he always knows when to get me up, even if I just dozed off. I believe God understands the craziness of my life and therefore He has to make a scheduled time to spend with me. I have found myself looking aimlessly in my dark bedroom trying to fall back to sleep after nursing Tamar. I usually toss and turn several times before I look at the clock and realize that it is my time to spend with God. It is during this 3a.m. wake-up call that I jump up so quietly and go into the living room to talk to God. I quietly shut the bedroom door behind me and I find my way to Blake's room and close his door to make sure I don't wake him. I make sure that my time with God is uninterrupted and that I don't disturb others of their precious sleep. I have to remember that I have to listen out for Tamar's cry so that she doesn't wake my husband during this alone time.

In the living room I have a drawer where I store my Bible, note pad, and a pen for easy access. I start out thanking God for allowing me to see another day. I follow that statement with asking Him a question as to what He would like for me to read for the day. In getting acquainted with God I understand that this is done by reading His word, praying, and fasting. In my reading time it seems as if God turns my Bible the direction He wants it to go because He has a word for me. After reading several chapters of whatever book of the Bible He has stopped me to read, I research the information by reading my outline within the text of my Bible. I then begin to pray for guidance for what I am supposed to take away from the reading. There are times when I am guided to continue to read an entire book. There are other times when I am guided to simply read a verse. The one thing that I know is that I want to know God's voice and be acquainted with Him, and I will do whatever it takes to do so. I was recently guided to start to read from the beginning of the Bible. I have read Genesis before, but I realized that God wanted me to pay closer attention to some specific things. In my early morning reading of the Old Testament I outlined some pretty significant things that correlated with my life and some of the people and prophets of the Old and New Testaments.

There was a time that I was thankful that I knew God and was acquainted with Him personally because of the ordeal that I faced. We were expecting our sixth child in 2009 and it seemed as if everything was going fine with the pregnancy at first. I started having dreams about a lot of bleeding and at times I would awaken to check to see if I was in fact bleeding physically, I was not. I didn't know that soon after those dreams that I would face the reality of a loss that would hurt me to the core. One Sunday morning I was having some stomach pains and my husband and I decided to go to the ER to check on the baby. It was during the ultrasound that it was discovered that I was pregnant, but the embryo was not in the sac. I became nervous after hearing the news, but I was assured by the doctor that sometimes this is the case in that the embryo doesn't form within the sac until much later. I felt some reassurance, but in my heart I knew something was wrong. I kept believing and praying during this time that the baby was okay. I went to get maternity clothes due to my protruding belly bump and to make me feel that the pregnancy was still viable. In every sense of the word, I was pregnant. I hated certain smells, it bothered me to lie down on my stomach, and I craved certain foods. I went to a scheduled OB appointment and we discussed the lab work and ultrasound completed in the ER in great detail. My OB felt that I should have a repeat set of labs drawn and another ultrasound. At this time, I still believed that everything would be fine. I thought about other people who had to believe for their children and the ruler Jairus came to mind (see Mark 5:24-34 paraphrased). Jairus daughter had died and Jesus stated that she was only sleeping. I felt that my child was only asleep. Jairus had to make the decision to believe what Jesus told him was true or what was reported to him by his servants. I think it was easy for Jairus to believe because as Jesus was walking with Him he encountered the woman with the issue of blood and she was made well. There is not anything in that the text that suggests that the ruler doubted what Jesus told him. It does appear that Jesus sensed some fear in the ruler because he told him not to fear, but believe. It is when we are acquainted and know God on an intimate level that He can just speak a word and we will believe.

We went in for the ultrasound and I could immediately tell from the expression of the technician that something was wrong. The technician excused herself and went and got the doctor. The doctor came in, and sat down and informed us that our baby was no longer viable. There was no heartbeat or sign of life remaining. My husband consoled me, but I was hurting all over. I had to face the fact that the baby was no longer viable and make plans to have a DNC to have the baby surgically removed. The doctor wanted me to give more blood just to be sure before making any rash decisions. We went home and waited for the results and received the phone call that we didn't want to take. We learned that my HCG levels were too low to have a viable pregnancy, again I wept. I knew God was not going to let the child come forth and I had to let it go.

The big day had come and I had problems sleeping throughout the night before. I was not prepared to have that precious child taken from me, but I couldn't continue to carry a dead baby inside of me. I heard the voice of God speak to me before I went into surgery and He stated that He had to give up His only begotten Son so that we all may have life. In hearing God's voice I wept and immediately reconciled that I wasn't the first or last person who had to give up something precious. I woke up in recovery and I was full of anxiety. I looked to my right to find my husband sitting there weeping silently. He was weeping because I was hurting so bad physically and emotionally. My doctor came in the recovery room and shared the fact that she had multiple miscarriages and that God finally blessed her with two children, her words didn't ease my pain. Many people might say that I should have not acted so emotional because I already had 5 children, I would say to them any loss hurts. I finally went home and as I entered my bedroom to relax I looked up to heaven and said to God that I would serve Him no matter what I went through. I told Him that He was faithful always.

As soon as we realize that it is not about us, we can move and operate in the power of the anointing of God. It may be that you have to get up at 3a.m. to get more acquainted with God in the quiet of your living room. You have to make a choice that you will sacrifice time, sleep, and whatever else to stay connected to God and to know His voice. Many people have told me that they want to know God as intimately as I do, but it will cost you. I find that many people just babble because they don't want to count the cost of getting close to God. Don't get me wrong, I enjoy sleeping especially when Tamar allows me to doze off, but in order for me to enter into the presence of God I have to respond to his wake-up call regardless of the time He selects. If you are seeking to know God and to experience Him move in your life, I challenge you to be open to His will and schedule. It's not always easy to find the perfect balance in life, but I promise you if you make an effort and give God quality time He will do the rest.

To Distinguish and Recognize God's Voice
is to *Know* Him

In our busy lives we have so many different sounds around us. There is the sound of the alarm clock. There is sound of horns beeping in traffic. There is the sound of an ambulance for emergencies. There are the sounds of laughter, crying, and mourning. The fact that there are so many sounds and people speaking we must know how to distinguish and recognize God's voice from them all.

There are many people who may approach you and tell you an idea or two that might be enticing. There are some ideas that are good, but are not from God. I hear people loosely using God as a way to get a point across. I also hear people saying that God is speaking to them almost 24 hours a day. I hear some who act like they have a direct line to God and that He is always speaking to them about other people and never about themselves. I beg everyone to distinguish and recognize God's voice although you are busy, tired, and at times too lazy to pray and seek His true will for your life.

Jesus knew the voice of Satan versus what God had spoken to Him about when he was in the wilderness for 40 days and 40 nights (see Matthew 4:1-11). Satan attempted to tempt Jesus when He thought He was at His weakest. Jesus didn't just sit back and allow Satan to misquote a scripture, but rather He was able to quote the scripture correctly and not buy into Satan's deception. We often don't know how to distinguish or recognize the voice of God because we are listening to other voices. We are listening to the defeating words of Satan. We are listening to family and friends and their agendas instead of knowing the voice of God.

There was a time when I had to distinguish and recognize God's voice from my own and that of Satan's. I believed that God prompted me to do some things that seemed out of character for me and others around me. We had recently built a large home in California and were working hard to decorate it when I believed that God spoke to me to make some drastic changes. This home was beautiful and had all the fixings of a California Spanish-style home. I ordered all types of expensive furniture to fill this beautiful home with. I finally got the home the way that I wanted it within 3 months of moving in. I was up one night praying and I heard God say that I was to give away everything in my home with the exception of my kids' beds. I won't lie; I thought that the enemy was trying to set me up. I was then prompted to take out paper and pen to write down each piece of furniture that I was to give away to a specific person. I was also told to give away computers, televisions, and all of the other gadgets collected over time. I was told that I had to call all these individuals the next day and inform them that they could have the specific items. I was scared and confused because the house was newly built and I had just finished decorating it. I was told that I was to put my home up for sale and the amount that I was to sale it for was given to me by God. I was told that I would be guided to where I would buy my next home.

The next day, I called all the people on the list and inform them that I was giving them certain pieces of furniture. Many of these people were speechless due to unbelief of what they were hearing. They all knew the quality of the furniture and the cost that was paid to decorate my home. I explained to them all that I was prompted by God to give them furniture. I also told them that I was moving, but I didn't have a clue to where I was going. God showed me in days after that a family of four would buy my home. He showed me that it would be a husband and wife along with an elderly couple. I simply put a sale sign in the front yard and left it there. I didn't advertise the home and I didn't use a realtor. You have to know that I lived on a cul-de-sac and there was little to no traffic in the area. One day after arriving home I noticed a small piece of paper stuffed in the door. I read the note and it stated for me to call because this person wanted to see my house. This did not happen overnight and I was beginning to doubt that I heard the voice of God telling me to do this. My furniture was all given away and God had already led us to the house we were to buy. I needed the money from the sale of the home in order to buy the new home we were building. I called the number and spoke with a gentleman and arranged for a showing of my home. The doorbell rang and there stood a husband and wife and the wife's elderly parents. I was so amazed because God had already showed me that it would be that way. As they viewed the home they immediately wanted to put in an offer. They even gave more earnest money then what I requested to make sure that I wouldn't sale it to anyone else. Remember, that I said God told me the amount to sale the home for, well, the home was appraised for the exact amount that I was asking, not a penny more or less. Since God told me to sell everything He must had a plan for me to get new things for the new home.

For the new home I was able to get everything I wanted and customize some of the pieces. I had to have faith and put action with it because none of that would have happened for me. I heard the voice of God and responded. It was because of my response and effort that God moved on my behalf. That was probably one of the strangest things I had ever done. There were some Nay Sayers who believed that it was the enemy who told me to do such a thing. I tell you though, when God speaks, He backs up everything that He says. It is not easy going with the unknown, but distinguishing and recognizing the voice of God will guide you. Don't worry about what people will think, say, or feel about you. It might have looked foolish to many when I did such a thing, but the blessings I received in the end just were overwhelming. The new home was built from the ground, it was bigger, had numerous amenities, and in a golf course community. Essentially, God upgraded me to another level. I am so blessed that God is still speaking and moving.

To Recognize God's Voice is to *Know* Him

John 10:14 (paraphrased) Jesus states that God is the shepherd and knows his sheep and is known by the sheep. This means that we are recognized by God and that we are to be able to recognize Him as well. Jesus goes on to say in John 10:27 that we as the sheep hear his voice and it is familiar to Him and this result in us following Him. The key to this verse is that we should never want to follow after a voice that is not recognizable. The problem is that we follow after the voice of Satan because we are not listening for the voice of God. We buy into Satan's defeating words and believe what he says about us. For example, the Bible teaches us that we are strong and when we are confronted with a situation we immediately start listening to Satan when he says that we are too weak to get through the situation. The Bible is our tool to helping us know and recognize the voice of God. The Bible teaches us that Jesus carried our sicknesses and disease to the cross and paid the price for our life. This doesn't mean that we don't need doctors. I believe that there are times when God shows up and make the report from the doctor insignificant. The tests may say one thing, but God shows up and does another thing on our behalf. The key is to recognize God's voice because it just might save your life.

I often hear people say that they get confused about recognizing the voice of God or if it's their own will. In getting up to spend time alone with God I have learned to recognize His voice from my own. I mentioned in the previous chapter that I would challenge you to sacrifice some time so that you get familiar with God's voice versus your own because it is essential. There were many people and prophets in the Bible who heard the voice of God speak to them. These individuals had to decide to follow God's voice or their own. I know that a lot of times or should I say most of the time it is easier for us to follow what we know and believe. The problem with following after our own desires is that we are flesh and spirit and there is always the urge to do what feels good versus what is good for us. Genesis (17 paraphrased) is the chapter in which Abram's and Sarai's names were changed to Abraham and Sarah by God. Abraham had to clearly recognize the voice of God telling him that he was changing his and Sarah's names and making a covenant with him. I am almost positive that Abraham would not have recognized the voice of God clearly if He had not positioned himself to do so. I know that there were days that he was busy as a leader and traveling to places God sent Him, but he had to stay in tune with God's voice.

Abraham recognized God's voice when he promised him a son with his wife Sarah although it seemed farfetched to him. Abraham also recognized God's voice when he told him to take Isaac, his promised son to the land of Moriah to sacrifice him (see, Genesis 22:1-19 paraphrased). Abraham recognized God when he told him not to slay his son. This is a moving and significant part of the Old Testament because to me it established trust in that God knew that Abraham was willing to give up anything for Him because he recognized and knew the voice of God.

I recognized the voice of God in the summer of 2001 when I had a life-threating illness. I had been visiting on the East Coast and after arriving back to my California home I was very feverish and lethargic. I assumed that I had a bug from the travel and wasn't immediately alarmed. It was after two days of feeling fatigue and the addition of a new symptom of my neck being stiff that I became a little concerned. As I attempted to fall asleep on the 3rd night of my illness I recognized the voice of God when He told me to go to the ER immediately. I responded to God and asked what I would say to them because my symptoms didn't appear life threatening. I recognized the voice of God a second time when He told me that I had to go immediately and that He would get the glory. I arrived to the ER and it was filled with really sick people. I almost felt that I was being insensitive for showing up with a stiff neck and a slight fever after seeing how many people were waiting. I finally got called to be triaged and was asked what was going on by the nurse. I explained to her that I had a stiff neck, felt fatigue, and had a slight fever. She informed me that it would be a long wait because my symptoms were not life threating.

I finally heard my name being called by the charge nurse and was elated that my over 2 hour wait was almost over. The ER physician came in and decided that since I had a complaint about my neck that he would order an x-ray. He informed me again that it would be a wait because there were others worse off than me. The x-ray technician finally came to get me and proceeded to take all the x-rays needed on my neck. I was taken back to my ER bed and heard over the loud speaker stating that they needed an ENT doctor to the ER stat. I didn't think that they were calling this person for me. My doctor walked back into my room with more doctors and stated that I was the sickest person in the ER. They immediately started an IV with morphine to help decrease my rapid heart rate because I was in pain, but I obviously didn't feel the intensity of it. I was rushed to the CAT-Scan room for a second opinion of what was found on the x-ray. This was all happening while I still didn't know exactly what was found on the x-ray. After the CAT-Scan, I learned that I had 5 pockets of fluid in the soft tissue area of my neck. This fluid is equivalent to aneurysms. They were life threatening because once they burst they could travel immediately to the heart or brain and the chances for survival is almost nil. They sent the chief doctor in to explain all this to me in between my tears. I wasn't comprehending what he was saying to me, so he grabbed me and looked me right in the eye and stated that I would die if I didn't allow them to perform emergency surgery immediately. He told me that my diagnosis had a high mortality rate. He proceeded to call for an operating room and gather a team of doctors who could operate on me in a delicate fashion so that the pockets wouldn't be disturbed. As he left me alone in the room crying, I looked up to heaven and the recognizable voice of God spoke to me.

God stated that I would see Him move by His power in that situation. He told me to tell the doctors that I was refusing surgery and that they should use steroids to treat me. I said, "Lord I am allergic to steroids", He answered that He was moving by His power and we all would see a miracle. The doctor returned and I informed him to call the operating room and cancel the emergency surgery. The doctor immediately grabbed me and stated that I was going to die if I didn't have the surgery immediately. I went on to ask him to treat my condition with steroids. The doctor explained that my condition could not be simply treated with steroids because it was life threatening and that would take time, and besides that, the condition has never been treated with steroids. I stood my ground and refused the surgery. The doctor informed me that I was allergic to steroids and my decision was against medical advice. I told him that I would sign a release for refusing the surgery, but I needed him to try the steroids. The doctor finally agreed under the condition that I would not eat or drink so that I would be prepared for emergency surgery at any time if my symptoms worsened. I was wheeled to my room and all of my vital signs decided to take a turn for the worse. My white blood count started to rise and I became very feverish in an attempt to fight the infection. All of my veins started to collapse making it difficult for me to receive the steroids intravenously. I had been poked all over my body when they decided that I had no other choice but to get the surgery. I asked them to have someone try to get the IV back in one last time, they agreed. They asked the anesthesiologist if he would try to find a viable vein. The anesthesiologist made it clear that he would only try once because all of my veins were no good due to dehydration from the fever. God showed up once again and he was able to get the IV running again. The fluids start to run and as the night went on my fever began to break. I continued to pray and believe God for a miracle that he had spoken to me earlier that day. By the next morning, the doctors were making their rounds and when they got to me they put an instrument through my nose that had a camera on the end of it to check the size of the pockets. This instrument provided a clear picture of the pockets of fluids I had. The first doctor looked and was totally amazed by what he was viewing. He had all the other doctors look and they were all amazed that these life-threatening pockets had shrunk in size. They explained that steroids were not something that they used for the condition. They decided that although I wasn't out of the woods, but that I was progressing I could continue to the steroid treatment. I was feeling better and getting stronger each day. I was finally able to go home after 6 days in the hospital. To this very day when I tell other doctors that I had a deep tissue infection they immediately look for a scar on my neck, but there isn't one. I challenge you once again to recognize and know the voice of God and act on what He says because it could very well save your life. Jarius acted on what Jesus told him in that he believed the word spoken about his daughter. I am not saying be foolish and not adhere to what your doctors tell you. I am saying that you will recognize and know God's voice versus your own when things work out the way that He said they would. The key thing to remember is that God wants the glory in all situations. He told me that I would see a miracle and He would get the glory in that situation, it happened. The one thing that I didn't mention earlier was that there was another man in the same hospital with the same condition on life support and things didn't look favorable for him. As one nurse called me her hero for fighting I could only look to heaven and thank God that I recognized and knew His voice so that He could get all the glory in the situation. God was the hero in this case, He just allowed me to play the part. I don't wear the usual scar for this condition because I never received physical surgery, but supernatural healing by God.

To Discern the Character and Nature of God's Voice is to *Know* Him

God will never lead His sheep astray and that is the beginning of discerning the character and nature of God. God wants what is best for His children. If we know and understand that it is not God's desire to see us sick, broke, weak, unstable, and confused we know that it is not in His character to take pleasure in us struggling in any of those areas. God will never have us to do something that is the opposite of His character and nature. God is love and He wouldn't expect us to walk in anything but love. God is longsuffering so He wouldn't expect us to walk in impatience with others. As we discern the character and nature of God we will want to be more like Him in what we say, do, and how we react to people and situations. I know that there is also this human side of us that hurt and mourn for things, but with God storms don't last forever. However, as we put more on the character and nature of God we will know His voice when He tells us that weeping may endure for a night, but joy will come in the morning. The character and nature of God is not to complain, but there are many times that we complain although God has spoken to us about His plan for our life. We are a people who want to see the proof in the pudding before we believe that it's real. Jesus' disciples had to discern that the time for Him to give His life on the cross was approaching, but due to their relationship with Him they couldn't and didn't want to let go. They didn't hear his voice when He would speak about His death and things to come because there was an attachment. It is not easy losing someone you are close to. There is no pleasure of seeing your love ones suffer or die. Jesus had to give up His will so that He could do the will of the Father. Jesus recognized that is was not His will but the will of His father. Jesus also wanted the cup of death to be removed from Him, but He was able to discern that there was a greater purpose for His death and resurrection. I had to be a position of discerning the voice of God when He told me that my brother was going to die over two years before he actually died.

I had just delivered my 4th child and had only been back in America from Cuba less than a year. There was no word that my brother was ill and as far as I knew everyone in my family was doing well. I was driving to take Asia to her appointment and I began to cry in the car. The cry that I had was not something that I ever heard before. The cry took on the sound of mourning and I became inconsolable while driving. I pulled over the first chance I got and I looked up to God and asked Him why I was crying. God spoke to me and said that I was mourning for my brother. I immediately got a little snappy with God and responded that I had four brothers and asked which one He was referring to. God told me that my older brother Eddie was going to die. He went on to tell me that I was to lead Eddie to him and if I didn't that Eddie's blood would be on my hands. I was so outdone after the whole ordeal. I had no strength to drive and I was literally shaking. My first thought was who in the world I could tell this to. I certainly couldn't tell my mom that one of her children was going to die. I couldn't tell my siblings because I didn't want them to think that I was crazy by saying that God spoke to me while driving. Please keep in mind that Eddie was not ill at this time so, it didn't make sense to me that he would die because he was in his early thirties. I went home and started praying and God spoke to me again and told me to cry then because He was my shoulder. In essence, God allowed me to cry two years in advance because He knew that I would be strength for the rest of the family when Eddie actually died. I finally got the courage to call Eddie and asked him about his health and caught up with the details of his life. I didn't hear anything alarming that made me feel that he was dying. I asked him about his relationship with God and according to him it was fine. In one of my conversations with God he told me to tell Eddie that his past righteousness would not be remembered. You have to understand that it was Eddie and my older sister Renee who encouraged my mother to go to a church that was on fire for God. It was at that church that my mom accepted the Lord and changed her life for the better. So, in essence Eddie was once in a relationship with God, but the cares of the world and following after the lust of the flesh he was no longer following after God at that time and that's why God wanted to point it out that Eddie's past righteousness would not be remembered if he didn't repent.

One weekend my mom and step-father went away to Michigan for the weekend and when they returned home they found Eddie nearly at the point of death. He was able to crawl up the stairs and immediately collapsed on the floor. He was rushed to the hospital and was put into the intensive care unit. My mom didn't know what was wrong with her child. I was informed of the situation

and all I could do was keep the secret that Eddie was
going to die from everyone. My mom couldn't get any
information about what was wrong with Eddie because he
informed the hospital not to tell her about his condition.
After he was well enough to go home, his condition didn't
improve and my mom continued to take him back and
forth to doctors. Finally, a nurse asked my mom if she
really knew what was wrong with Eddie and my mom
informed her that he told her that he had a blood
disorder. The nurse reluctantly informed her that he
really was dying of AIDS. The nurse took a chance by
telling my mom Eddie's true condition because she could
tell that my mom didn't have the truth from the many
conversations they had. It was after learning that Eddie
had AIDS that I was able to make sense of what God
spoke to me in my car.

Eddie's condition grew worse because he was so
concerned about being discriminated by others that he
wasn't receiving the proper medical treatment. He was
only receiving care from a family physician and not from
an infectious disease doctor. Eddie continued to go on
with the lie that he had a blood disorder. Eddie's shame
seemed to have influenced my mom because she also
chose not to disclose Eddie's true illness until much later.
My mom didn't call for the Elders of the church to pray
as the Bible teaches us to do because of the shame. She
didn't have anyone come and anoint his head with oil
because she didn't want to be judged for her son's actions.
She basically carried the burden of her oldest son dying
alone. My mom solely depended on her relationship with
God and a few family members to help her through that
rough time. I believe that she didn't want to be looked
down upon for her son having a disease that was linked

widely to the gay community by the media and full of myths as to how it was acquired. In essence, she suffered in silence for a long time.

Eddie decided that he wanted to move to be near the ocean in the last days of his life on earth. He asked me to find him a home in Virginia Beach where I lived. He came out and we found him a place that was comfortable. Eddie decided to start to going to church with us and there is where he found some individuals suffering from AIDS as well. This church had a grant from the CDC allowing it to have and conduct an AIDS ministry. Eddie met another young man who inspired and encouraged him for the remainder of his short days remaining on the earth. The pastor of this church took our family under her wings and nurtured us all. Eddie joined an AIDS support group and found the right type of doctor to help him manage his disease progression.

For a short while it appeared that Eddie was on the right track of getting better. He no longer had to spend time hiding his disease and found other people to socialize with who would not judge him because they were all in the same boat. It was after leaving church one Sunday that Eddie felt he was having a difficult time breathing. I took him to the ER and learned that his lungs had collapsed from fluid building in them from complications of AIDS. Eddie became worse and it looked as though that he was at the end of his precious life. I called my mom in Chicago and informed her that she must get to Virginia soon because Eddie was not well. My mom arrived soon after and she was really hurt by the decline in Eddie's health. As I left the hospital one day I began to pray in the Spirit and God spoke to me that Eddie would die on a Sunday. He told me that I would lead Eddie to Him and that he would be saved.

At this point my mom decided that she wanted to relocate to Virginia Beach as she transitioned into her new home it appeared that Eddie once again cheated death. As the months went by and the fall leaves began to fall Eddie became sick once again. I began to have dreams that Eddie was disappearing. I soon felt an urgency to lead Eddie to the Lord because I believed that he was going to die soon. As I picked my children up after school one day the Lord prompted me to go to my mom's house and pray with Eddie and lead him to Him. It seemed as though days earlier that each day I went to the home Eddie was in a deep sleep. I rang my mom's doorbell and when she opened it she was in tears because she received a call from the doctor that Eddie's brain was shrinking at an alarming rate, this was a complication of AIDS. Eddie already decided early on that if he died that he didn't want to be resuscitated. I immediately went upstairs and Eddie was sitting in a chair just staring at the walls. I asked Eddie if he wanted to be saved and he shook his head yes. I told him to repeat after me and he did exactly what I asked. I also gave him (Romans 8, NKJV) that states that there is no condemnation for those who love the Lord. Eddie needed to know that his past sinful life would no longer be remembered by God and that he was a new creature the instant he repented. Eddie went on to ask me to read him a few verses, and I obeyed. In doing all of this it would seem unlikely that I would be the one who God chose to lead Eddie to Him because we didn't have a close relationship. It seemed to me that no matter how nice I was Eddie always had it in for me. I had to remember that in knowing God I had to discern the character and nature of God and not have my agenda with Eddie but God's agenda. I had to have longsuffering, love, kindness, gentleness, and all the other fruits of the Spirit (see Galatian 5:22) if I was to confess that I knew God to Eddie.

I didn't know that would be the last time that we heard Eddie speak from his mouth. The Bible teaches us that we are to confess with our mouth and believe in our hearts that Jesus is Lord and God raised Him from the dead in order to be saved (see Romans 10:9), Eddie did that. Eddie was in a coma the very next day and unable to speak. I firmly believed that God knew that Eddie would be comatose the next day and that was why the urgency to go to the house and pray with him was necessary. We decided to call all the family to Virginia Beach because Eddie was not improving. It was once all the main members of the family arrived and said their peace, Eddie was free to go home and be with the Lord. As I mentioned earlier that the Lord told me that Eddie would die on a Sunday, well, Eddie rose up from his bed early Sunday morning and took his last breathe. The cousin who was in the car with me when I spoke that word over a year prior came to me and stated that today was Sunday just past midnight. I tell you to know God is to discern His voice and it will surely come to pass if it is Him speaking. I had to overlook the insults, the negativity, and the disrespect that would come from Eddie in order to fulfill the purpose that God had for him. I was just a willing vessel and decided that I would put on the character and nature of God in order to know His voice when He told me to do something for the advancement of His kingdom.

Chapter 2

Hearing God's Voice

There are many things that we hear throughout any given day. We might hear the phone ring or the doorbell buzz. We might hear the sound of music or the television. We might hear our children call our name because they hurt themselves. We might hear the sound of the ocean as the waves toss back and forth. We might hear the voice of God speaking telling us to get up and pray about a situation even if we don't fully understand why. Hearing is defined as: to listen with attention, or to perceive or apprehend by the ear. This means to me that you have to be focus in order to hear correctly.

My aunt heard the voice of God prompting her to pray for her husband one day. She responded to the voice of God and stated that she had already prayed for him that morning during her daily devotion time. God spoke once again for her to pray. As she prayed for God to keep and protect her husband she was unaware that he needed her prayers at that very moment. My uncle was driving down the busy highway in Chicago when his brakes went completely out. He had to react fast and get off the highway to prepare for an accident. As he called on the Lord and made a few maneuvers God responded and allowed the car to come to a complete stop without injuring him or anyone else. You see, it is so important to know God because it positions you to hear from Him. Noah heard from God when he told him to build the ark (see Genesis 6:13-22). I could imagine that it looked so foolish to be building a large vessel like the ark, but nonetheless, Noah heard from God and responded. Noah and his family were saved because he heard from God and follow the instructions given. Noah had to first know God before he could hear from Him. The Bible says that God saw Noah as righteous (see Genesis 7:1), which means Noah knew God and therefore was able to hear from Him. There were many times that I heard from God because I already knew Him, but as a teenager I didn't always pay attention to His voice.

To Listen to with Attention is to *Hear* God's Voice

I mentioned in the previous chapter that I have six children, but the path to them getting here was not easy. India, my oldest child had to fight for her life while in the womb and when she came out. I was only 17 years-old when I became pregnant and gave birth to her. I was an unwed mother and I was very alone during that time. I realized that I committed sin by having sex before marriage, but I wasn't prepared for everyone to turn their backs on me. I solely had God to talk to during this time. My mother, a strong Christian woman, felt that I brought shame to the family and decided not to allow me to attend her church with her anymore. I assumed that she didn't want my pregnancy to have a negative impact for her as a parent. I cried to God in my pillow almost daily and asked Him to be there for me and to help my child. Our neighbor and friend decided that I could attend church with her and that was what I needed. As the message went forth it seemed as if God was talking directly to me. I felt that He was saying that regardless of the mistake that I had made that all was forgiven and that I had purpose and so did my child. I went into labor at only 26 weeks pregnant. I was sleeping after a long day and night of not feeling well. I woke up to find that my amniotic sac had ruptured. I started shaking uncontrollably because I knew that was not a good sign. I woke up my mom and told her what was happening. She woke up my step-father and they immediately drove me to the hospital. I wasn't prepared to go through such an ordeal alone. My parents dropped me off in front of the hospital and drove off. I was rushed back to a room in the ER to confirm if indeed my sac ruptured, it did. I was crying and I needed God more than ever at that moment. I didn't have family or anyone familiar with me. I was wheeled up to labor and delivery to prepare for the child to come into the world. The doctor informed me that she was underweight and that she might not survive. The plan was to try and keep her inside the womb for as long as possible to allow her more time to grow. I was doing fine for the first few hours there, but I soon took a turn for the worse. My amniotic fluid became septic to my body and I developed a high fever from the infection. The doctors wanted to continue to watch my progress but things got worse. My temperature spiked to over 105 degrees. My unborn daughter's heart rate was very faint. I was alone and desperate to hear from God. As I lied there I heard God say that it will be all over in the morning and that I didn't have to worry. I told God that if He allowed me and my daughter to live that I would raise her to know and fear Him. Things became very critical for me and the baby. I was told that I had 50% chance to live and that my baby had less than 1% to live. The doctor put out a code as they raced down the hall with my bed. I looked at the doctor and asked him if he thought I would live and he stated that he would try his best to save the both of us. Some might say that this was a lot for a young girl to go through, but God was with me. I didn't have anyone from my family to hold my hand or to tell me that it would be okay. I only remembered them putting the oxygen mask on my face and I fell asleep. I woke up and realized that I was alive and as I struggled to get my words out, I could only utter words about my baby to the nurse. She informed me that she had to call ICU and find out the status of my baby. She found out that my daughter was gravely ill, but that she made it. I was too weak from the infection to ask anything else. The story of Hagar reminds me of what I went through with my pregnancy from the aspect of feeling alone and shunned.

Genesis 16 talks about Sarai encouraging Abram to sleep with Hagar her maid servant so that he could have a son. Sarah at the time didn't believe that God would allow her to have a son of her own so she decided to go the surrogate route. My story reminds me a lot of Hagar who was shunned away by Sarai and fled to the wilderness while she was pregnant because she was humiliating Sarai about her ability to conceive. Pregnant and alone I am sure Hagar was afraid just like I was. While in her wilderness experience Hagar heard the voice of the Angel of God speak to here and tell her that she must return to Sarai and submit. The Angel also told her that she would have a son and that she should name him Ishmael (meaning God hears). Because this child was a seed of Abraham he was still blessed and Hagar was promised that her descendants would be too many to count. I think this story is relevant if you're pregnant or not in that God is with us even in our wilderness experiences. This was one of two times that Hagar would leave and find herself in the wilderness.

Genesis 21:1-21 talks about after the birth of Isaac that Sarah wanted Hagar and her son sent away once again. Abraham was not in agreement with this at first because Ishmael was his son. However, God spoke to Abraham and he heard Him say that he should do what Sarah asked of him in letting Hagar and Ishmael go. God told Abraham that Isaac would be called assure Him that he had purpose. Abraham had to yet again put himself in a position to hear God. Abraham heard God say that although Isaac was the one called that He would still make a nation of Ishmael. I believe that hearing God's voice in such a crucial time of letting your son go off into the wilderness gave Abraham a sense of peace that everything would be okay. It was when I heard the voice of God tell me that India would be okay that I knew that regardless of all the obstacles she faced she would come out victoriously.

Hagar was alone with her child in the wilderness when she heard the voice of God speak once again. Hagar had used all the food and water that was provided by Abraham for her and Ishmael and she believed their only fate was death. Hagar cried and her young son lifted his voice and God heard him. I don't think there is a good mother on this earth who could stand back and watch their child die and there is absolutely nothing she could do about it. As they cried the angel of God called to Hagar from heaven to bring her words of comfort. The angel of God told her that her son would not die because the voice of the child reached the heavens. The angel informed her that Ishmael would be a great nation and this meant that he would not die, but live. God opened the eyes of Hagar and she was able to see the well in front of her. She was able to give her son the water he

needed to survive. The Bible goes on to say that God was
with Ishmael. I feel the anointing of God as I write these
words because I know that God was with me and India
along the way. India became stronger and stronger each
day until the day she made it to five pounds and was able
to go home. Keep in mind that her brain bled many
times, her lungs collapsed, she needed multiple
transfusions, and I was told that she would not be normal
because her nervous system was not fully developed.
Well, I have a testimony for all of you. India is healthy
and has her right mind. She is one of the most intelligent
people I know. She graduated from high school at 16
years old while taking college courses. India is a college
graduate and has a desire to serve people within the
medical field. India is left with the scars of all her IV
pokes in her hands and feet. I believe that God did not
allow those scars to fade to keep a reminder that He was
with her in the wilderness and that He heard her cry.
There is no mention that Hagar was angry or hated Sarah
and Abraham for their actions of sending her away. I
know many of you would think that I have malice in my
heart towards my family, I don't. It took God to heal my
heart and I was finally able to forgive them. You might
ask if they ever asked me to forgive them, the answer is
no. I don't need them to ask me for forgiveness because I
want to walk in the freedom of forgiveness and love so
that I can continue to do the work of the Lord. I can't
flow in the power and anointing of God if I have
unforgiveness in my heart. Please, if you have any
unforgiveness towards anyone, this is the time to let it go
so that you walk in the freedom that God has called you
to be in. There are situations in life that occur in which
we see the mouth of someone moving, but we are not

perceiving or apprehending what they are saying with our ears. Could it be that we tuned them out or what they are saying is not effective? As we read the Old and New Testament there are countless verses where God states that individuals are not hearing with their ears. In order to know God's voice you have to perceive and apprehend by ear what he is saying.

To Perceive or Apprehend by Ear
is to *Hear* God's Voice

God referenced throughout the Bible how the children of Israel refused to listen with their ears. In Ezekiel 12:1-2 the Lord spoke to Ezekiel and let him know that he was surrounded by rebellious people. God stated that they had eyes to see and ears to hear but refused to do so. There are many people who have received a word or words by prophets, preachers, teachers, and by anyone sent by God and they refused to adhere to the message. In reading Ezekiel God had him do a lot of strange things that we all probably would have rebelled against. God used Ezekiel in many cases to show Israel how displeased He was with them and also for things to come. There are cases when my children didn't listen to me and had to learn the hard way about certain things. They later returned and stated that they should have listened in the first place. I think that if we all had an ear to hear we would save ourselves a lot of time and heartache. God has always used me in the area of the prophetic and word of knowledge. I have never been one of those prophets who promised people a new house and car. I never had a name it or claim it ministry. I have lost family and friends due to the words God have given me to speak

There was a time when God showed me that a relative of mines house was falling off its foundation. I prayed and asked God what did my dream mean and if I should only intercede on her behalf or should I warn her. God informed me that her physical house structure was not falling down, but that things in her life would crumble if she did not turn back and serve Him. I gathered up the strength to call her and tell her this warning. As I finished the conversation she became very angry at me and asked me who I thought I was to give her a word from God. She immediately hung the phone up in my face. I was shocked and hurt that she responded in such a way being that she used to have such an incredible relationship with God and He spoke to her on a number of occasions. I just continued to keep the matter in my heart and prayed for her. As the winter approached I learned from another relative that the relative's husband left her one day while she was at work. She was devastated about the situation. She has since had issues with her only child and I am often reminded about the phone call that took place and how she turned a death ear to the warning. I think that the reason so many Christians find themselves in the same place spiritually after walking with God for so long is because they refuse to hear His voice. Jesus often spoke in parables and people were often confused as to the meaning of them. The parable of the sower is a great example of people who hear, but they don't perceive or apprehend.

Matthew 13:1-9 details the parable of the sower. In this parable Jesus describes the sower and how he went out to sow and found some of the seed had fallen by the wayside, some on stony places, some among thorns, and some on good ground. The ones that fell by the wayside are individuals who hear the word and it is immediately stolen from them. To me these individuals don't allow the seed planted to penetrate. This is the case for many people. They run to God when things are going bad and they hear the word on Sunday morning that encourages, inspires, and empowers them to change, but when things improve they go back to doing what they were doing. I used to be this type of person in that the seed would be planted but trying to fit in my environment I found myself forgetting about the seed planted. The ones that fell on stony ground are the individuals who have no real root planted in order to be preserved. I have learned in order to grow in the kingdom of God I had to invest time in the seed planted in order to gain some depth. I believe my growth came from reading God's word and hearing Him speak to me through it. The seeds that fell among thorns mean that these individuals are mixed in with the weeds and are being overtaken by them. I believe that when you have a seed planted by God to do His work you must be willing to change your lifestyle. You must be willing to change the people you run with, the things you do, and the places you go. There must be a distinct difference between Christians and the world. I am not saying that we won't interact with non-Christians, but our character must be different to the degree that they can easily distinguish a difference. There are a lot of us who talk the talk, but we are not willing to walk the walk and be the examples we should be for Christ. Finally there are some seed that fell on good ground and this mean that these individuals hear the word of God and run with it. They encounter struggles and obstacles but they are so planted in their relationship with God that they continue to thrive regardless of what happens. They don't throw in the towel every time the wind blows. They don't turn on

God because He doesn't respond immediately to their requests. They don't practice sin and be accepting of it. They have a relationship with God that is not based on emotions or circumstance but rather a solid relationship that is the result of trusting, hearing, and knowing God's voice. They are not perfect, but are working toward striving for perfection.

Paul heard the voice of God speak to him while he was on the road to Damascus (see Acts 9). Paul had been against God and his people for a long time when God met him on his journey of what he thought would be furthering his agenda to persecute Christians. Paul believed that what he was doing was right and justified. He thought that he was doing what was right in his own sight and that of his people. Paul didn't know that God had a plan for him if he would simply hear his voice on that road. Paul was told by God to go into the city and he would be told what he must do. The Bible says that the men who were with Paul on road heard the voice, but saw no one. This is what we encounter when we read the word of God and hear it in our hearts but see no one. The word of God is to be heard and we are to do what it says in order for the seed within us to continue to grow. God is willing to meet us where we are. It could be on a road, hospital, in the car, or in your home. We have to position ourselves to hear His voice and respond. I thought it was interesting that Paul acknowledged Jesus as Lord when he asked him why he was persecuting Him. This means that although Paul had his issues, he knew and acknowledged the voice of Jesus on that road. As Christians how much more so should we be hearing and responding to the voice of God. Paul went on to do many things by the power of God. A lot of us want to move in the power and anointing that the book of Acts speaks of, but we are not willing to put ourselves on the road to hear from God. We have our own agendas and we are a right now society. I urge you to get on the road to hearing the voice of God because you just might get to know Him intimately.

Chapter 3

Obeying God's Voice

God is speaking today like never before. Some might say how does he speak? God speaks through His word, through you, and He sends others to give you a word from Him. It is not so much how and when God speaks, it's you willing to obey His voice when he does. In raising our six children there are many times that we have told them to do this or that and they didn't obey. They for whatever reason failed to obey due to having their own agendas or because they wanted to rebel. The fact of the matter is that when we obey God's voice there is no chance for us to go wrong. In obeying God's voice this doesn't mean that we won't be confronted with opposition. The first time we are confronted with opposition we are quick to say that maybe we heard God's voice wrong or that God couldn't be in something because there is opposition. Obey is defined as: to follow the commands or guidance of or to conform to or comply with. In order for us to obey God's voice we have to be willing to follow His commands and guidance. We also have to be willing to conform and comply to His will. The struggle that most of us have is that we enjoy doing things our own way. We don't want to have to be told to do things. We feel as adults that we are mature enough to make the right decision. However, I believe that spiritual maturity is vastly different than physical maturity. We can test this in how we pray. A lot of times when I didn't know how to pray I used to beg and plead God for things that I personally wanted and thought were beneficial to me. As I matured as a Christian I now pray for God's will to be done in my life. It is not always comfortable obeying the voice of God, but in the end we realize that it's for our best. There was a time when I had to obey the voice of God when we got stationed in Central California in 1999 and it wasn't easy to do so, but it was one of the best things that I had ever decided to do at that time.

To Follow God's Commands or Guidance
is to *Obey* His Voice

In early 1999 God showed me a dream that we were moving to CA from Virginia. I thought that it was impossible due to the size of our family and how the military didn't commonly move such a large family to an area with such a high cost of living. The area God showed me was surrounded by palm trees and the sun was shining. It was a beautiful place to behold and it was San Diego. I shared my dream with my husband and he informed me that would not be possible due to our family size of relocating to that area. After speaking with the military and discussing orders he learned that they only had California available. I was not shocked at all after he reported back to me that we were moving to CA. The only catch to this story was that it wasn't San Diego that they were moving us to, but Lemoore California. I had never been to that part of California and I didn't know what to expect. I just remembered what I saw in my dreams and I was holding on to that. We packed up the car and headed west and as we were driving into our new state and city I started getting discouraged because the scenery didn't look at all like my dreams. I started to wonder if I missed something in my dream or my conversations with God. It looked like I was in the wilderness. There were no palm trees, but the smell of cows, sheep, and pigs were infiltrating the air. I was crying just about the view of the area. I told God that there was no way that I was going to live in that place. I kept complaining and crying and one day while driving I heard the voice of God speak to me and told me to stop complaining. God said that He sent me there to do a work and that I couldn't hear or see because I was too busy complaining like the children of Israel. I started to cry as I heard these words. God went on to say that there were souls there who cried out to Him and that He heard their cry. He told me that I was sent there to lead people to Him. He told me to start a women's group and I was to meet the women in different places. My first thought was I don't know a soul here. My second thought was do God expect me to go up to random strangers to get this group going.

Well, as I stopped complaining I was hearing God speak so specifically. I heard Him speak to me and told me to buy invitations and I was to hand them out to the women He pointed out, that was hard for me to do. In my obedience to God I would approach different women in stores and other places and invite them to my home for Bible talk and lunch. These women were all random and I had no relationship with them prior to my approaching them. I went up to roughly 10 women and I also asked a neighbor I just met while moving in to join us. The big day came and all the women I invited showed up. Prior to their arrival God told me specific things about these women that I would have not known. I wrote all that He commanded me to write down about each of them. He told me to share these things after I was done with the meeting. I prepared lunch and spoke the word that God had given me. I then shared with each lady the things

God had given me. You would have thought someone had died in my home with the amount of tears shedding from each of them. They all were in awe about the things that God revealed about them that they knew I could have not known. This Bible study went on faithfully each week and started to grow. The women would invite others to come with them. I led people to Christ and I was in total peace. I don't believe that I would have had any peace in Lemoore if I hadn't obeyed the voice of God and followed His commands for me there.

As the summer went on and souls were being blessed and saved God told me that we were moving again. I asked God how that was possible because we had only been in that place 3 months. I reminded God that the military don't move families twice in the same fiscal year. God once again spoke to me and told me that Lemoore was simply a detour because He heard the cry of the people. He told me that I obeyed His voice and that my work there was completed. He told me that He was sending us to San Diego. I didn't jump up in down because I thought that we were going to San Diego the first time. Well, we received word that we had to move because they made a mistake in sending us there in the first place. They said that they had to move us to San Diego. There was no fuss about the money that they had already spent sending us cross country or the money that they were about to spend. You see, when you are willing to obey the voice of God and follow his commands and guidance anything could happen. If I would have kept complaining and didn't do what He asked of me lives could have been potentially lost. I didn't want the blood of those people to be on my hands. It is easier to obey God then to follow after your own agenda. It looked strange to me approaching total strangers but God knew what He was doing. These women were so blessed and encouraged from the word that God sent weekly. If God is willing to speak you have to position yourself to obey. In order to obey God's voice you have to be willing to conform and comply with what He tells you to do.

To Conform and Comply to God's Voice
is to *Obey* Him

It is not always an easy decision to conform and comply with what others want. In our relationship with God it is not a good idea to do things our way. I always had been a big advocate of people having their own minds and making their own decisions. In the spiritual world we have to learn that it is not about how we want to do things but what God requires. There is a time when walking with God that a choice must be made if you desire to get to know Him on an intimate level. There are many good Christians who are going to make it to heaven, but I don't believe that they will walk in the fullness of their anointing or call if they don't conform or comply with what God wants them to become and do. I don't want to simply make it into heaven but I want to walk in the power and anointing of God on earth. I want to comply and conform to the person He wants me to be so that His kingdom is advanced. I have tried countless times to do things my way, was disappointed. I tried having my own agenda and at times be rebellious to the call on my life, didn't go well. It's much like when you get married and the two of you become one. You can no longer have your own agenda and do things your own way. You have to listen to, and at times, with comply with the requests of your spouse. There was a time when I had to conform and comply in order to obey God's voice. It was during a church service that I was attending that I heard God speak to me about a woman in the church. First of all, I was new to hearing from God and I considered myself a bit shy back then. The shyness and my unfamiliarity with the woman almost caused me not to conform and comply with obeying God. However, I heard God say to be that obedience was better than sacrifice.

I heard God tell me to let the woman know that she must seek Him and His kingdom and not worry about anything else. He went on to say that if she put Him first everything else in her life would line up. Keep in mind while reading this that I didn't know this woman and I was visiting that church that Sunday. A great fear came upon me and I wanted to not comply at all. I was thinking that what if this woman thought I was crazy. What if she was already seeking God and that everything in her life was on track. What if I was simply wrong! I kept feeling the urge from God and finally I gave in. I tapped the lady on the shoulder and stated what God told me. The lady just looked at me as if she was in disbelief that I approached her at all. There was an intermission time and the lady asked me to come into the hall with her. She was weeping as I approached her and she explained her situation to me. She told me that God had given her the scripture the same morning where it says to seek Him and His kingdom and its righteousness and all else will be added (see Matthew 6:33), the same words I told her in the sanctuary. She explained that she had been going through so much with her family and asked God to send her a sign so that she knew that He heard her prayers. I give all the glory in this and take none for myself, but I was yet amazed how God once again used me. I first had to be willing to conform and comply to be obeying His voice. If I allowed myself to conform to fear I would have missed out on the opportunity to bless this woman who was desperate to hear from God. If I would not have complied with his request this woman could have never found the peace that she was seeking at that moment to help her make some life changing decisions about her family. The Old Testament talks about Saul and how he decided that he would do things his way. He decided that he was not going to conform or comply with obeying God's voice. God was not pleased with the way Saul was doing things.

I Samuel 13, 14, and 15 outline the life of Saul and how he refused to obey God's instruction. Saul did unlawful sacrifices that were not of God and was warn of such by Samuel. Saul was made a rash oath that backfired, he continued the war that was supposed to stop, and he spared King Agag. For his actions and his desire not to conform and comply with obeying God's voice Saul was rejected as King. The think here to ponder is that if we are unwilling and refuse to obey God will raise up someone else who will be willing to conform and comply with obeying His voice. Saul was so desperate to hear from God that he consulted a medium (see I Samuel 3:3-25) to get direction and guidance. God is longsuffering, but he doesn't make us doing anything against our will. He doesn't force us to serve or obey Him. There are times when I believe that we know we are out of His will and that is why we become weary and restless. Saul also had distressing spirits on him because he was out of the will of God. I was distressed prior to writing this book. I couldn't sleep and I was very restless each night. I knew that God wanted me to write this book, but I felt that I had too much on my plate already.

We just relocated to Southern California due to military orders and I just had a baby. We also had to settle into our new home and my office was getting organized. I thought how in the world I can fit writing into my busy schedule. I was looking for a nanny and someone to help with the home. I kept making excuses until I finally gave in to obeying the voice of God. It has never been my desire to write a book because after completing my dissertation I said I don't want to have anything to do with writing. However, the more I rebelled the worse my sleepless nights came. I explained to my husband what God wanted me to do. He immediately responded that I must do what God has asked of me. He agreed that he would watch the children each day after he gets home and allow me to write in the bedroom. I still wasn't convinced that I was doing what God required of me. I was thinking what if God wants me to do something else and I didn't hear Him correctly.

Well, I called a friend of mine who I haven't been in contact with regularly to let her know that I had the baby and moved. As I told her about getting settled she interrupted the conversation and stated that God wanted me to write a book and to finish it quickly. I literally almost fell out of my seat because I only shared what God said about writing with my husband. I started crying and thanking God that He once again allowed me to hear His voice and know without a shadow of a doubt that He told me to write this book. My prayer is for everyone to look within themselves and see how they can know, hear, and obey the voice of God regardless of the circumstances, obstacles, and other distractions you might have. It is not easy for me to conform or comply to obey because I have my own agenda that I want to adhere to. I thought that I would come to Beverly Hills and start seeing clients immediately, but God has other plans for my life. I can sit around and complain, rebel, and refuse to obey if I want to, but in the end I will suffer. I don't want to be like Saul and find myself seeking a word when God already is speaking to me. I want to walk in the freedom and obedience so that my relationship with God is intimate. I don't want to be unforgiving to others because that will block my blessings and prevent me from hearing from God.

I believe that God wanted me to write this book to free me all the more and to share my experiences with other so that they can see that we are all overcomers through Christ Jesus. I pray that this book will inspire, encourage, and empower you all to go on to do great things because you know, hear, and obey the voice of God. I also hope that mothers who read this book will be encouraged to spend time with God to hear from Him regardless of the number of hats we sometime have to wear. I sense that there is an urgency like never before to walk in the fullness of the spirit of God. In this hour God is speaking but are we listening. We must position ourselves like never before to know, hear, and obey God's voice because of the time we are living in. I pray that a hunger and thirst will come over the body of Christ like never before to hear from God and seek His direction for the church.